Death B   taches

by: L.T Greyson

Death by a Million Heartaches

L.T. Greyson

Published by L.T. Greyson, 2025.

Copyright © [2025] [L.T Greyson]
All rights reserved.
No part of this book may be reproduced without permission from the author.

While every precaution has been taken in the preparation of this book, the publisher assumes no responsibility for errors or omissions, or for damages resulting from the use of the information contained herein.

DEATH BY A MILLION HEARTACHES

First edition. February 7, 2025.

Copyright © 2025 L.T. Greyson.

ISBN: 979-8230742647

Written by L.T. Greyson.

Table of Contents

A Note to My Readers 1
A Special Note to My Friend Sydney 2
Acknowledgments 3
Foreword 4
The Nightingale's Song 8
How will I die? 9
In The Wake Of Melancholy 10
How Do I Stop Caring? 11
Ink Of the Forgotten 12
I Needed A Hug 13
Behind The Facade 14
Depression Is The thief Of Joy 15
A Knock At Death's Door 16
Dancing On Needles 17
Echoes Of Shattered Glass 18
Haunted 19
Sands Of Time 20
The Intruder 21
Mosaic Of A Broken Heart 22
Untitled 24
The Weight Of Your Absence 25
Inheritance 27
Family Isn't Family 29
My Mother's Distant Lover 31
Untitled 2 32
Thorns of Devotion 33
Crimson Echoes 34
Untitled 3 36
The Worth of Me 37
The Cardigan 39
Hoax 40

Wildfire, Wild-love	41
EVEN	42
Violent Devotion	43
Untitled 4	44
Hunger	45
Jealous	46
Shades of Distress	47
Michelangelo	48
Untitled 5	49
The Mind	50
Epiphany	52
Mirror	53
Weak	55
Untitled 6	56
Love breeds heartbreak	57
Unraveled	58
The Gods of Time	59
Echoes Of You	60
Fragments of Us	62
A Tender Hoax	63
The Art of Dying	64
Failing	66
Perfection is illusive	67
Oblivion	70
Chains of deception | I loved a boy once—	71
The Soul is a Garden	73
Skin Deep Wounds	74
Andrew	76
Shadows of Unhappiness	78
To be loved , But Not.	80
Untitled 7	83
Desire in the void	84
Delusions of a worn out heart	87

Seventeen years of grief..91
Abacus of Injustice..93
Dear Future Me,..95

A Note to My Readers

To anyone and everyone who has or is about to embark on this journey with me, I thank you dearly for your support and time. I dedicate this book to the voiceless, the little teenagers who cry themselves to sleep, and most importantly, to anyone who has ever felt the need to read or write poetry—or use art in any form—as an escapism, a means to express their deepest, innermost feelings and cope.
YOU ARE SEEN, LOVED, AND VALUED.

A Special Note to My Friend Sydney

I cannot express enough gratitude for your unwavering belief in me. You have been my rock, my biggest motivator, and cheerleader, especially during times when I felt like my work wasn't good enough or worth any attention. When my world felt like it was collapsing, with the man made walls closing in on me, you were there to help me break right through them, encouraging me to keep going and reminding me of my worth. Your support has meant everything to me, and no matter the state of our friendship by the time you're reading this, I dedicate this book to you. This is as much yours as it is mine. Thank you for being my constant source of strength.

Acknowledgments

I would like to take a moment to express my deepest gratitude to those who have shaped my journey and inspired the very essence of this book.

First, I would like to thank Taylor Swift. Her music has been my sanctuary, healing me and guiding me through times of struggle. Her ability to express raw emotions through melody and lyrics has deeply impacted me, and her art has helped me find the strength to keep writing.

To Emily Dickinson and Sylvia Plath, your poetry has been a beacon of light in the darkest corners of my mind. Your words shaped my art and taught me to embrace vulnerability in my writing. You have shown me that there is beauty even in the most melancholic of moments, and for that, I am eternally grateful.

Thank you to all the artists, creators, and individuals who have believed in me and supported my work. Your encouragement has been my driving force.

Foreword

"Death by a Million Heartaches" is more than just a collection of poems and prose; it is a reflection of my journey as a Black, gay boy navigating the world of self-discovery, love, loss, and healing. Growing up, I always felt like an outsider, caught between the complexities of my identity and the world's expectations. My skin, my sexuality, and my creativity all made me different, and at times, I struggled with how to reconcile those parts of myself. It wasn't always easy to find a place where I felt seen, heard, or understood.

I didn't start writing poetry until I was 16, but creativity has always been a part of me. Music was my first form of expression, my way of connecting with myself but it wasn't until I found poetry that I was able to translate the same feelings into a different form—a more intimate, raw exploration of the emotions that had been swirling inside me for years.

Writing poetry became my refuge in a world where I felt too often misunderstood. Through the years, I wrestled with mental health struggles—feelings of isolation, confusion, and an overwhelming sense of not belonging. But in the quiet of my own space, I turned to words as an escape. Poetry gave me the freedom to explore the deepest parts of myself, to share the vulnerability I'd often kept hidden away.

Being Black, gay, and a creative person means that my perspective is unique. It has shaped how I view the world, how I express love, and how I understand myself in relation to others. This collection reflects those layers of my identity—from the raw emotions tied to my experiences in a world that can be unkind to people like me, to the empowerment I found in embracing my flaws, and to the catharsis of expressing my creativity. Poetry allowed me to merge all these identities into something beautiful, something that was mine, without apology.

The poems within these pages are an exploration of the pain and growth that come with being different in a world that often seeks conformity. They are stories of heartbreak, resilience, and self-empowerment. Through poetry, I've learned that my experiences—though sometimes filled with heartache—are valid, and that there is beauty even in the darkest of moments. This book is for anyone who has ever felt like they didn't fit the mold. It's for the misfits, the outsiders, the misunderstood. It's for the ones who feel like they have to fight to be seen and heard, for the ones who, like me, are navigating their own journey of self-love and acceptance. I hope these words offer you comfort, understanding, and the reminder that you are not alone in your struggles.

Publishing this book at 17 is one of the scariest things I've ever done. It's hard to put such personal work into the world, knowing it might be judged, misunderstood, or dismissed. But this is the challenge I've chosen, and I'm embracing it, even in the face of fear. I've learned that sometimes, the biggest leaps of *faith come from the moments we are most unsure. If this book speaks to even one person, if it helps someone feel seen or heard, it will have been worth every step.*

I hope this collection resonates with you, not just as a reflection of my journey, but as a mirror for your own. I invite you to join me in embracing our differences, finding strength in our vulnerabilities, and celebrating the beauty that comes from simply being ourselves.

Love is Death to a Broken Soul.

The Nightingale's Song

Depression
The nightingale that
sings eerie melodies,
jolting me from my sanctuary—
the warmest place I've ever known.
Her tunes linger on,
and on, and on,
even when she's nowhere
near the visible horizon,
leaving behind traces
of uncertainty
for the foreseeable future.
She soars higher,
in blue—
skies vast enough
to paint perfect portraits,
portraying my patronizing
paralysis.
But all that does to me
is pin me down,
so low my soul shatters
to pieces like fragile glass,
actively fanning the flames
of my misery.

How will I die?

My mind drifts away at night,
When the world is fast asleep.
How will I die?
Will it be by a million self-inflicted cuts,
Or by your love?

In The Wake Of Melancholy

Why I dwell on my soaring melancholy,
Will eternally be the most unparalleled
Enigma to me.
My heart is truly a paradox;
It craves one thing,
To be adorned
Yet it derives pleasure
From its own misery.
Unravel the complexities
Of my soul ,
leave it uncloaked,
Leave it be free -
Free of armaments and mechanisms
All aimed at keeping it concealed.
But only for a while,
Only until I evanesce
Into the abyss of my mind.
Oh pardon my language
But fuck,
I find it all very uncanny to me-
The concept of being in a world
Merely driven by the lust of mankind.
Kind men all perished from the face of the earth,
Earthly motives coop my conscience
In a place most undesirable .
And, so I ponder;
The question that begets itself:
"Why do I dwell on my melancholy?"

How Do I Stop Caring?

How do I stop caring?
How do I stop pouring my love into broken vases?
Is it my fault I give too much to
People that don't see me for who I am
And too little to those who do?

Ink Of the Forgotten

Somewhere in my eyes,
A warning cry lies,
Hidden in plain sight.
Don't wanna die,
But I hate being alive .
So I'll carve caskets
On my wrists
With the blade
In my fingertips,
"Death" engraved on my lips.
Crimson glaze oozes
From the hands
Of an innocent soul
Forgotten,
Once known.
A canvas painted
With the ink from my veins.
Demons once chained
Now run wild like the fear
That engulfs my mind
In the wake of the night.
Terrors arise inside,
Outside the errors
Linger like a shrouding shadow.

I Needed A Hug

I didn't need trauma
To give me strength,
Or toughen me up.
I didn't need character development.
I needed a hug.
For God's sake, I was a FUCKING CHILD.
I needed to feel loved
And comforted.

Behind The Facade

Most people see me
as this ecstatic being,
but what they don't see
is the covert animosity
I harbor against myself,
the wordless wars waging within.
But what if I burned the facade
I put up every day?
What if I tore down the walls,
shining light to the indentations—
my precious scars, so indelible?
Would the world see me
for me?
Would they embrace my flaws,
or shy away,
petrified of imperfection?

Depression Is The thief Of Joy

Depression is the thief of joy,
Robbing me of glimpses of happiness.
He creeps up on me when I least expect it,
Right when I've found healing.
And he leaves me asphyxiated,
Gasping for air.
A captor—
He keeps me hostage,
Hidden from the world
Behind his sharp walls of misery.
I could never break free from his prison,
Even if I tried.
His lingering persistence
Instills fear in me.
And if I ever dare
To rise up, like a phoenix
From the ashes,
He pins me down
And whispers in my ear:
"Till death do us part."

A Knock At Death's Door

Why do I have to
fall into the depths of despair
for people
to believe my distress?
Do I need to incessantly
gash into my skin
for everyone to eye my melancholy?
Surely I could just knock
at death's door
and he'd let me in.
Maybe then the
mournful paradigm
I'm in would cease to exist.
It's not pity I crave,
nor is it a savior I need.
It's the final termination
I'm direly indebted to.

Dancing On Needles

It feels as though
My heart is waltzing on needles,
Each beat steadily shadowed
By the haunting melody
Of the blistering pain.
Every step takes me
Closer to insufferable consequences,
Carrying me further
Away from reclaiming the
Pulverizing peace I once knew,
And yet, I still dance.

Echoes Of Shattered Glass

Shattered glass ruminates,
Gleaming on the floors
That once reflected my
Thoughts like a mirror.
Mirror that bore
Morphed shadows
of my broken soul.
But what if the
striped silhouettes,
Etched on my skin,
Are just remnants of wars
waged deep within?
Deep within the abyss,
Within the walls that
Echo pain
walls that spell
Out your name
On my bluest days.

Haunted

After giving
every inch,
every haunted corner
of my body,
the skeleton
of my soul,
what more
is left
to give?

Sands Of Time

The stars in my eyes
Like constellations
On a lonely night .
The blood on my hands
Drained from my old self .
The guilt in my smile
Ignited by the trauma
Of my past life .
Am I too weak?
Or is the world too heartless?
Maybe I'll be there
To find out
In another lifetime .
But I'll leave this all behind
Leave this pain
Leave it be washed away
By the Sands of time.

The Intruder

My body
Doesn't feel
Like mine anymore.
I feel like an
intruder in my own skin.
I can't recognize the soul
Staring back at me in
The mirror.
Could it be because
It's not me?
Just another version of me
From an alternate reality
I cease to exist in?

Mosaic Of A Broken Heart

Just like glass
A shattered heart
Can never be pieced
Together again.
The sentiment of it
All lost-
It's fragments scattered
Like a lonely mosaic,
or pieces of a puzzle
That no longer fit together.
Pour love into
It's cracks
And it'll leak
Through the
Littlest seams,
Draining itself
Until it's empty

What's The Point of Living If I'm Just Going to Die?

Untitled

Is my body
Just a public sanctuary?
Does it not belong to me anymore?
Does it not hurt you hurting me?
To go in and out of it as you please?
Surely if I had a choice ,
If it was up to me
I'd have not been born
And bred into a world this cruel.

The Weight Of Your Absence

In moments like these,
When my mind slows down,
I ask myself:
What would life be like if you had stayed?
Would things be the same?
Would I still be weighed
Down by this pain?
It haunts me murderously
To think about how I see so
Much of me in you.
I, too, hide away
At the first sight of trouble,
Cloak myself in my little bubble,
Where no one can have access to me.
Does my misery entice you?
Does it coax you into utopia?
Does it not keep you up at night?
The thought of my pain
Being such an imposition?

I was art
He was visually impaired

Inheritance

My inheritance,
My curse,
My beloved anchor.
Its weight stunts my growth.
I carry my mother's rage.
I bear her incessant urge
To unravel herself
For the benefit of everyone but her.
Her guilt seamlessly flows into me,
Like charges of current passing through a wire—
Inescapable.
My father's shame banes me:
His desperate need to vanish,
To sever ties with love.
I, too, suppress my emotions,
Keep them hostage,
Until they detonate—
Ticking time bombs.

CURSE MY INHERITANCE.

Don't forget to save a bit
For yourself-
The love you pour out to
Undeserving souls.

Family Isn't Family

Family isn't family
When water is thicker
Than the venom
That runs in their veins.
Sometimes a stranger's
Love is bigger than that
Of those you share
A last name.
Holding onto them is
Like rubbing poison to
An aging wound,
Watching it eat my life away-
Dolefully decaying
As I dwell on my dismay,
Heavily betrayed
Like unsuspecting prey
And not expecting
To feel any pain.
But letting go-
Oh,
letting go
Is the sweetest
Salvation,
the remedy
Of a soul
Slowly shattered
By words they said
Or actions expressed.
MY LITTLE LIFE'S BANE.

My Mother's Distant Lover

I remember you.
I remember...
I—
...shouldn't have to beg you to be in my life.
Seventeen million years and prayers later,
My bloody knees have grown minds of their own.
Still, they grind against the earth,
Hoping—
Hoping you'll save them
From their inevitable collapse.
You're like the sun
Close yet far away
But still you
Actively burn me with
False hope
Promises of a world
That seems to be centered around
Your presence.
YOUR ABSENCE HAUNTS ME.
Your light shines upon and burns me
Simultaneously.

Untitled 2

A part of me still wonders
If you ever truly loved me.
Because if you did,
You wouldn't have replaced me
So easily, so quickly.

Thorns of Devotion

But I'd set my heart ablaze
Before you get the chance to
I'd water you with my love
till it overflows
Cause I never know when I'm giving
Enough, too much
Or just the right amount
If you told me that you loved flowers
I'd garnish my soul with carnations
So you could love me
I'd destroy every part of me,
Soak every fibre of my soul
In acidic thoughts of you
For you I'd run on thorns
Feel them prick me,
As my brain idly reforms
The pain into something
More tolerable
Something more alluring;
Your love
I'd taste the sweet kiss
Of death just for a glimpse of your smile .

Crimson Echoes

Tear me apart,
In the most gruesome way.
Cloud me in agony.
Touch my soul gently,
Like I'm a canvas,
Canvas waiting eagerly
To be your next victim.
Shape my thoughts,
As each brushstroke
Trickles down my spine.
Splatter me with paint,
Or better yet, acid.
To me, it's all the same.
Savour every moment,
Manipulate my heartbeat
Till the heavens collapse on us.

Loving you brought
      Me glimpses of heaven
            And eternities of pain.

Untitled 3

Do I truly love you?
Or am i lost
In the distorted perception
Of you
That I've created
in my mind?

The Worth of Me

My heart pumps blood,
And gives out love for free.
My brain offers
Thoughts just for me.
My eyes work together
So I can see
The natural landscapes
And the sea.
My legs take me from point A
To point B,
And my hands craft
The finest poetry.
So why, then, should I care
About the acne on my face
Or the gaps in my teeth?
Is my worth
Determined by the flaws
Of my body,
Or by the
Love and immense gratitude
I pour out every day?

*The inexplicable urge
To express my feelings
Tends to get shadowed
By my sudden inability.*

The Cardigan

My heart is a battlefield—
Isolation, her bravest soldier,
Fighting relentlessly in wars
You began.
It is more than just a muscle;
My heart is a seed,
Flourishing in the coldest winters.
It's a flower
That can grow on ice,
Devoid of warmth.
Yet, it crumbles to pieces,
Fragile and yearning,
When deprived of your love,
Of your essence.
Without you,
My heart is as useless
As a cardigan
In the raging summer heat.

Hoax

Why do we have to wait,
Till after death to be coaxed
Into the utopia of the afterlife?
Is bliss on Earth unattainable?
Impractical?
Truly, it leaves me bewildered.
The oceans, forests, and stars
Are all a part of
The most alluring elements of nature,
Yet we overlook them,
Chasing promises of an uncertain heaven.

Wildfire, Wild-love

I desire what I cannot hold,
Yet hold what I do not need.
I need what's hidden—
Buried deep
In the chambers of your heart.
Love—
I crave love.
Wild love that engulfs me whole,
A wildfire,
Reducing every part of me
To ash.
Love that fuels me,
Yet destroys me,
Tearing down
The blue walls on my horizon.
Because that's the only love I know:
One that leaves me breathless,
Asphyxiated—
Deprived of air.

                                                        EVEN
━━

SILENCE

                                                    CARRIES

                    W
                    E
                    I
                    G
                    H
                    T

Violent Devotion

I devote my love to you, violently,
patiently waiting for you to consume me.
I watch as your
innocent eyes
slice my ribcage open.
What follows next?
Cannibalism—
in its purest form.
You take what's rightfully yours.
I sacrifice myself,
placing my being on the altar,
offering myself for your indulgence.
You bite into my flesh,
your lips look down on me,
red ink dripping from them.
But why do I endure this torment?
If I can't make you love me—
I, who am incapable of love.

Untitled 4

Sometimes butterflies
And burning signs,
Signal danger.
The adrenaline rush-
A warning mistaken
For love.
But you,
Oh you're so naive
BEGONE FROM THAT RELATIONSHIP
Flee from your misery.

Hunger

Most people fall in love,
Yet I disintegrate in it.
I burn in the flames
Of my lover's eyes.
My heart is hungry—
Hungry for affection,
But my soul craves something
That transcends
The metaphysical.
To be understood.

Jealous

Oh and I'm jealous-
Jealous of your scars
Cause they'll stay with you
Forevermore,
Bound by the threads of destiny
But I can't.
Isn't it mortifying?
The way your name
Fills every corner in my mind,
Chapters in my books
And stanzas in my poems,
But mine is merely the
Ink on your pages.

Shades of Distress

Painted my canvas red
With nothing but
A silver blade.
The blush increases with
The intensity of the brushstrokes.
Each stroke, a silent sigh,
Muffled cries,
Hoping for someone
To hear, see, and feel
The shades of distress
That bleed
From my tortured soul.
The scarlet pools—
Museums of anguish,
Filled by my essence—
The fusion of rivulets
And the ink I spill on pages
Nobody will ever see.
Pain meets poetry
For desperate moments
Of release.

Michelangelo

My body is the rarest
Form of art—
Poetry at its finest,
Sculpted by the same hands
That shaped David.
It radiates angelic melodies,
Ringing with tunes of perfection.
So why do I bare it to predators,
Who crave nothing
But to tear it apart—
For fleeting glimpses
Of gratification,
Moments of self-pleasure?
Perhaps I savor the attention,
Because it's the closest thing to love
I'll ever know.

Untitled 5

Hold on to that little
Ray of sunshine.
Keep it hidden
Deep in your pocket
Save it for that unprecedented
Stormy day.

The Mind

The mind is like a tree
Your reality Is dependant upon the growth
Of this tree
Every branch reflects a single thought
Be it positive or negative .
When the positivity
Precedes the dark
A positive reality is manifested.
But should negativity
Take root-
It stunts the growth
Of the mind.

Are you really in love
Or is your heart just distracted?

Epiphany

And maybe
the purest form of love
Is one that can't be reciprocated.
How beautiful is it to love someone
Without expecting anything back?

Mirror

Body to body
Skin to skin
Nothing fills
The void within.
Starved myself
Made friends with pain
But nothing heals
Quite like that blade.
Can't fight the shame
That lives inside
When guilt invades
My fragile mind.
Comfort seems
So out of reach
When people say
I've gained.
When skinny
Isn't good enough
And my body's out of shape.

Still I hold on
To a time
When his gaze
Wasn't as flawed,
When his judgment
Spawned from my
dear truth
And not from
Worldly views.

Weak

How dare you blame it on me?
How dare you call me weak?
It was not my choice to be abused.
Neither was it your right
To gruesomely take away my innocence .

Untitled 6

This quote haunts me
More than I'd like
"If you keep telling yourself
That you're depressed,
You will become depressed"
So I'll keep telling myself I'm over you.

Love breeds heartbreak

For one to truly experience heartbreak
They first have to experience love
For heartbreak is essentially the
Void
Left
Behind
once
Love
Is
Gone.

Unraveled

I didn't know
how broken
and hollow
I'd been inside,
until I let a stranger
unravel
my body.
Thread by thread,
every nook and cranny—
each knot slowly
untied
with merciless care.
Not for love—
not for attention,
but for proof.
Proof that I
was capable
of being seen
for what I was,
even if only
for a fleeting
moment.

The Gods of Time

If loving me
Brought you hell,
Would you walk
Through the flames
With me?
Or would you
Sit and
Watch me burn and turn
To ash,
Enveloped in clouds
Of amber?
Am I deserving of your love?
Do our souls dance to the same melody?
Or does mine ring frequencies far beyond
Your reach?
Our synchronistic bonds
Blown away by the
Gusts of destiny—
The gods of time?

Echoes Of You

My heart still echoes
Your name.
I still save space for
You in my brain—
Space vast enough for you
To flood my thoughts
With violent shades
Of your essence.
The stars in my eyes
Don't shine as bright
In your absence.
I miss you, unfathomably,
Incomprehensibly,
In a way that haunts
Me to sleep.
That's where I ever see you anyway—
In my dreams.
Loving you is like
Watering plastic plants,
Hoping they'd grow,
Clinging to the illusion
Of something real.
But maybe if I gave just
The right amount,
They'd bloom into a garden
Of memories,
Ones we're yet to make.

Love is the essence of a beautifully maimed heart.

Fragments of Us

My heart pumps
Words I'll never say to you.
My lungs respire
In scents of you.
My brain thinks
Solicitously of you,
In ways inexplicable
To everyone else.
Yet all I am to you
Is merely the last thought
That engulfs your mind.
My soul shatters in half,
Impatiently waiting
And waiting
AND WAITING
For you to put it together
With your bare hands—
The same hands
You use to camouflage
Me from the terrors
That lurk beyond our
Fragile haven.

A Tender Hoax

The sun sinks its teeth
into my organs of sight,
burning its light
with pure delight
onto them.
Still, I admire it,
gazing upon its rays
with peak confidence,
without a fright,
capturing the essence
with my blemished sight.
Somehow, it reminds me of love—
the piercing sunlight,
both beautiful and bright,
crippling, blinding, if you may,
in the dawn of day.
Love burns not my eyes
but my soul—
a tender hoax
that leaves me blindsided,
unable to make wrong
or right of things.
And yet I dare to face it.
I stand tall in the midst of it all,
and I call it beauty.
Truly, beauty is pain,
Pain is love, love is a game.

The Art of Dying

Just like music and poetry,
Death is also an art—
An intrinsic aspect of life,
Feared by many, avoided by none.
But to hold back is to
Deprive thyself
Of the liberation tangled within.
Why would I—
Or anyone with the apprehension
Of the dark and twisted human race—
Choose to stay?
Plead with fate?
Or gods of the like?
Death is inextricably
Linked to the peace
That comes thereafter.
But for many, the predicament
Is a fear of letting go
Or a lack thereof—
A maddening attachment
That ties us to our own adversity,
Like a mother to her unborn child.
Death is as much
A part of life as birth itself—
Much like peas in a pod,
Inseparable, like
The sun and moon,
Love and heartbreak,
Yin and yang.
Two opposing forces

That somehow complement each other.
The same way a horse gets tethered
To a post,
Similarly, life is tethered to death.
How beautiful is it
To lay down on the earth that birthed you?
To be caressed by her soft tentacles
That stretch out for miles on.
To be one with nature,
One with being.

Failing

For every time you fall,
Ask yourself:
Is this a minor setback or a major comeback?
Losing hope should never be an option.
It won't always be easy,
But never give up.
Be strong.
Get back up,
Dust yourself off,
And rise again.

Perfection is illusive

Perfection is illusive;
she's a shapeshifter,
bending towards
societal standards.
She's a pressure-tropic
response to the advancement
of humanity and technology.
She's a pest,
a parasite that thrives
on her host's dismay,
draining it of the little
self-worth it has left.
She is like ivy—
widening the cracks
of a broken soul,
amplifying concealed insecurities.
Alluring at first glance,
but tremendously poisonous
when left untreated.
Perfection is a malady,
an incurable ailment that
masks unsightly souls
with the facade of a "beauty"
that is unattainable.

If nature is exquisite,
yet still flawed,
what then gives us

the right to be perfect?

Love is the catalyst to my inevitable disintegration.

Oblivion

A select few want to know
how their death will be served.
Others seek the details
of their final moments,
but my soul aches with a question
that haunts me endlessly:
In whose arms will I take my last breath?
Some fear heights,
others the dark,
and some, still, the notion of what they call "homosexuals."
But my deepest fear is far greater—
the fear of dying unaccomplished,
of leaving no trace,
no memory of the change I was meant to bring.
I fear fading into oblivion,
dying without ever knowing
if my life meant anything,
if I ever truly mattered.

Chains of deception

I loved a boy once—

A bloodthirsty beast who
Craved nothing but to
Make a meal of me,
Like a predator starved for days, weeks,
Even years.
He was a two-faced spirit,
Who lured me in,
Heaving me closer
With barbed wires of deception.
A bloody chest aching with infatuation,
I fell in love with the devil.
He made indelible incisions
Into my heart,
And hung it on his great wall of achievements,
Wringing it dry of the little love it had left,
As if it was his old pair of jeans.
And still, I loved him.
Still, I made excuses for him.
Still, I stayed.
I was one of many pawns
In his deadly game of chess,
And the more steps I took,
The fewer chances of survival I had.
But still, I was ahead of
All the other pawns.
A magnificent player.

I was under his control—
A lifeless puppet under the false illusion
Of love.
I was naïve.
I thought that was the kind of love I deserved.
I bled the last of my love for him,
But at what cost?
Now all that's left of me is an aching silence,
A void where love once burned.
And now, I roam the earth,
In pursuit of a new lover to fill that void.
I've finally been set free—
Like a bird from a cage.
Cut loose from all the ties
That once kept me tethered to him.
Yet, even in my freedom,
I still search for the safest place to land.
A love so pure it mends what's broken,
And heals the scars he left behind.

The Soul is a Garden

The soul is a garden,
Water is her remedy.
The foundation for her growth
Is dependent on rich soils,
Free from toxins that may prevent
Her from flourishing,
Or pests that may attach themselves,
Feeding on her energy.
Fertilize her wisely,
For that added boost is vital,
To make her flowers bloom beautifully.
Inspect every petal, ensure it's healthy,
And surrounded by flowers of the same kind.
Prune and deadhead wilted blooms,
For they interfere with the garden's beauty,
Leaving space for new life to emerge,
As she continues to expand her territory.
Take care of your soul,
Protect your energy,
Kill the weeds,
And let your spirit thrive.

Skin Deep Wounds

Maybe one day,
the magnitude of your unnatural desires
will inwardly collapse on you
due to your lack of remorse.
Maybe then,
your cancerous exploitations will finally
spread like a tumor,
growing uncontrollably, then consumes you.
You don't know how filthy I feel—
the kind of impurities
that cannot be washed off by praying
or by soaking myself beneath a shower.
It's the kind that lives within me,
that traces my every step
and reminds me of my unworthiness.
My skin violently crawls;
it tugs and pushes back and forth
like an old creaky cradle
In a haunted house,
a pendulum measuring
the weight of my shame.
It doesn't feel as comforting as it used to.
Now it loosely fits me like an oversized garment,
hiding the dirty secret
that whispers softly beneath it.

My skin utters weeping wails of disbelief.
It caves in on me
as if I'm not its natural bearer—

DEATH BY A MILLION HEARTACHES

as if I'm an intruder
who must pass various biometric authentication barriers
to finally be identified.
It shuts me out completely.
She fires missiles inwardly,
instead of projecting her fears
towards deserving perpetrators.
Her coping mechanisms are detrimental,
and as a result,
I am left locked out of my body,
keys nowhere in sight.
I am not one with my sanctuary anymore,
but only he's to blame.

Andrew

Your laugh supernaturally echoes,
In ripples on the surface of my body.
It's ghostly how
It leaves me possessed by your aching phantom.
Our memories pave a path so distinct,
I can almost feel your warm embrace
As I bolt on the blazing asphalt,
Fleeing from the incessant urge to
Go down your road.
My lips quiver in disbelief
When I hear your voice,
Singing our favorite song in
Digitized memories.
My heart, so blue.
My septum ruptures,
A million microscopic pieces
Chipping off
When I think of you.

Oh 'Drew,
Come back to me,
Rid me of this torment.
My days have become a paradigm—
An endless loop
Of the April when I lost you.
From long summer days
To piercing winter nights,
You still invade corners of my mind,

DEATH BY A MILLION HEARTACHES

And I still scream at gods in the sky,
On my bruised violet knees,
As I plead for your magical rebirth.
It never works.

Shadows of Unhappiness

I haven't know what true happiness feels like,
for as long as I've escaped the prison-like
entrapment I had been confined in for 275 days.
I am unfamiliar with the concept,
truly disconnected from it.
Could I have been born this way?
Or was it my own little adaptation to the harsh world—
my defense mechanism?
What if, the same way plants produce antimicrobial chemicals
to fight pathogens,
my body produces chemicals of the same kind,
but only to fight happiness?
Could my body truly repel something
that lives inside me?
An innate, universal characteristic of what it is to be human.
But I don't feel human at times.
It feels as though I don't belong on earth,
but on a distant planet where creatures like me reside and bathe in
their melancholy.
How fitting that is—the idea of having a place somewhere in the
universe
for tortured souls like mine.

I've spent my teenage years hating myself for being different,
for loving what it is that I love,
but not anymore.
I am who I am because I love what I love,
and that shouldn't make me any less desirable than anybody else.

I've grown immune to sadness;
I've found solace in it.
My soul aches with familiarity,
but unfortunately, the only thing it's familiar with
is this constant state of dread,
and I've found peace in acceptance.

To be loved, But Not.

To be loved is to be seen,
but I'm a lonely ghost,
trekking the highest peaks of the earth,
leaving no prints on her warm belly whatsoever.
I pass right through people,
dissolving into thin air.
Then, like a puzzle piece,
I reassemble,
my being put back together,
glued by the mysterious power I am yet to acknowledge.
To be loved is to be heard,
but my spirit sings soft melodies,
gentle whispers to the smallest trees.
The haunting tunes of the nightingale
overshadow my words,
leaving them no weight,
no life of their own.
My thoughts echo and bounce back and forth
on the tall indigo walls of my brain;
they never escape,
forever held hostage in a world so blue.
This shrunken heart of mine
screams lullabies of love to the fullest of its ability,
but, like everything else,
they get absorbed by the gusting winds.
To be loved is to be desired.
I'm an old vintage cardigan,
torn apart by time,

left to be vacuumed into the earth.
I'm a stray dog,
left to fend for herself,
going through life with no one by her side.
I'm the definitive product of melancholy, regret, and abandonment,
a child mistakenly born into this world,
neglected by my alcoholic mother
and runaway father—my creator.
I'm the paralyzing pain that stays with you,
attaching myself to the core of your being like a parasite.
I'm the malady that brings dread to society,
wiping out entire bloodlines, generations, nations,
and lingering long after.
I'm the crippling consequence that comes
once a drug has been misused by an addict,
or a child has been abused.
What would this world be without me?
The ever-burning flame of hell,
the Devil's spawn.
To be loved is to be,
and I am not.
I simply am not.

Untitled 7

If choice were truly mine, I would fully immerse myself in the world of literature, willingly drowning in every piece ever written by man.

Desire in the void

And I don't want to die
But how soothing would it be
To know that people care about me,
As I'm rotting in a casket
Six feet deep
Somewhere beneath the earth.
To finally have people pay attention to me
Without ever having to beg for it,
Without having to force conversations,
Or make small talk
With people that don't care about my well-being.
To have flowers of all kinds of beauty
Surrounding Me,
Growing above me.
Maybe I do wanna die
Or maybe I just want to be passionately loved,
To be put first above anything and everything
And everyone else.
That's what I need.
My deepest desire.

But to die means to leave it all behind-
The nothing I have ,
The legacy i failed to build,
The friends that never understood me,
The family that couldn't accept me for who I was fearing eternal damnation
By a God they pray to in the empty sky.
Or the children of mine I never intended on having,
Cause I wouldn't want to bring life to a place so undeserving of such a precious gift.

Delusions of a worn out heart

A lousy love is one I do not desire.
Why would I crave something so mediocre
When I could bathe in pools of
Your undying love?
The oceans of your adoration
Are what I swim in.
I'd trade lives with the swordfish,
Maybe even grow gills,
Just so I could soak myself forever in you—
Scouring the depths of your devotion,
As my breathless body
Beautifully sinks beneath your waves.
Oh, your love is what I breathe in.
Your love is what I bathe in.
Your love,
Your love.
It sets me ablaze,
Even when I am surrounded by monstrous
Volumes of water.
Your love burns me and leaves behind
An incandescent glow, bright enough
To light up even the darkest night skies.
It leaves an inexpungible mark on me,
Your footprints on my wet, cemented soul.
You belong to the stars, the galaxies,
But oh, I belong to you alone.
Innumerable life sentences gifted to me
By your precious heart—and I don't complain.

Is this what my life has led up to?
But I digress.
These are merely the delusions
Of a heart so worn out,
Vanquished by your love—
Shrinking, diminishing,
In your absence.

My propensity for self isolation is the cause of my despair.

Seventeen years of grief

If I fell in love with my insecurities,
my flaws—the reasons behind my internalized animosity—
would they also cut me loose,
break all bonds between me and them?
Would they also leave me like you did,
Father?
What gives you the right to call yourself one
when you've never shown the slightest bit of interest?
Does it burn you the same way it corrodes into my flesh—
acid to metal—
the haunting possibility, the illusory belief
that maybe, one day, you'll understand
just how much your absence weighs on me?
How much I sink in the rivers of sorrow I bleed out
from the desert in my eyes
when someone asks me about you?
Seventeen years of grieving a soul
that walks this very earth.
I'm exponentially growing tired.
But I'm aware, so aware,
detrimentally aware of the love
you vaguely give out like tokens—
tickets to my demise,
a movie you orchestrated
so perfectly,
with precision and meticulous care.

To what do I owe this pain?

Is my existence not the greatest punishment?
Am I not already tortured enough as is?
And though it all seems impractical,
I still hold on to the flickering beam of hope—
that one day, it'll burst,
a parade of light falling from the sky.
And that day,
you'll finally return.

Abacus of Injustice

Society glorifies abusers,
Hold them high up on a pedestal,
Disregarding the victim—
Her muffled cries, the unheard melodies,
Drowned out by the praise,
While she finds solace in the shadows,
The little girl who was preyed on by men,
Who reek of desperate starvation.
Their minds, planes of purgatory,
Her body—a mirror reflecting their brokenness.
So they punish her for their sins.
The guilt that lives inside
Burns her, a fire torched by the same men
That preach freedom and women's rights.
Yet, behind closed doors, when the world isn't watching,
They snatch the girl's childlike innocence,
Leaving her drenched in shame,
Her purity peeled off, stripped off layer by layer.
She freezes in terror
When he forcefully undresses her
And pins her to the ground,
Like a battered banister, painted beautifully in shades of bluish-grey by
the man in an attempt to disguise her bruised body.
A tremendously courageous girl,
Who keeps his nasty secret hidden beneath creaky floorboards.
The skeletons in his closet haunt her forevermore,
While he lives to torment other play dolls.
The cycle renews and spins round
Like wheels of a 1970s bicycle,
And with every turn,

Yet another victim is tallied,
With abacuses of injustice,
The system that let them all down.
Yet the blame falls on her
For "showing skin,"
Or not dressing her age,
While the man is excused—
His impulse to degrade,
Objectify, and silence her
Is ignored, brushed off like dust on his shoulder.
The same girl who trembles
In fear of what's to come,
A prisoner to his sins.
The same little girl whose youth is now no more
Than a quick feast for predators,
For those who know nothing but to
Hunt for what is forbidden and sacred—
Her innocence,
'Cause it's what she sought out
As normal her entire life.
Now, the hungry eyes of men tiptoe
On her freshly bruised skin,
Her voice goes unheard,
Her childhood taken away.
Her back stands flaccidly, worn out
From carrying the weight of his actions,
So perfectly, you'd think it was her cross to bear.

Dear Future Me,

I hope this note finds you well, happy, and thriving in ways I can only dream of right now.

Today, I'm sitting with a mixture of hope and doubt, trying to create something meaningful—poetry, art, a life worth remembering. I'm working hard, despite the moments of exhaustion, insecurity, and fear. Right now, the weight of the world feels heavy, but I'm carrying it because I believe in you, in the person I know you can become.

I hope you've kept that fire alive. I hope you've published the poetry book, made the music, and touched lives with your art. I hope you've found joy in the journey, even if it wasn't always easy. Remember, perfection is an illusion—you're enough just as you are.

Take a moment to look back and thank the version of yourself who wrote this letter. They believed in you with all their heart. Be kind to yourself, celebrate every victory (big or small), and remember why you started this journey.

I'm proud of you, always.

With love and unwavering hope,

17 year old You

About the Author

Lefika, who goes by the pseudonym L.T. Greyson, is a 17-year-old poet and writer from Botswana. His work explores the complexities of human emotion, introspection, and the delicate interplay between joy and sorrow. With a deep reverence for the power of language, L.T. Greyson crafts poetry and prose that invite readers to delve into the multifaceted nature of the human experience. Drawing inspiration from literary greats such as Emily Dickinson and Sylvia Plath, his writing captures the subtleties of love, loss, identity, and self-discovery.

Through his words, L.T. Greyson seeks to uncover the beauty found within pain and vulnerability, offering raw and honest reflections on the heart's deepest desires and fears. His writing is both personal and universally relatable, capturing the moments of life that resonate with us all. With Death by a Million Heartaches, L.T. Greyson presents his debut collection, marking the beginning of a lifelong journey of self-expression and creative exploration. Having long believed in writing as a form of self-therapy and connection, L.T. Greyson's work speaks to those who are navigating their own emotional landscapes, facing their fears, and finding strength in quiet moments of reflection. Each poem and piece of prose in this collection represents a step in his evolution as a writer, and he hopes these words will connect with readers, sparking introspection and offering solace to those who need it.